Copycat Recipes on a Budget *for Beginners*

Save time and money by recreating these 50 recipes by choosing quick and easy meals to prepare.

Gordon Benedict Richman & Ernest D.W

LOVE TO COOK

Table of Content

Introduction

Dear Reader,
My name is Gordon Benedict Richman. I'm an experienced chef with a passion for good food. With this book, I want to show you that you don't need a spell to prepare delicious lunches or dinners that taste just like those in great restaurants.

How about a tasty soup or a light appetizer before the main course? Or even as the main course? It doesn't have too many calories and doesn't weigh down your stomach. Plus, both can be cooked in advance and frozen.

What would a special meal be on holidays or weekends with only one course? Somehow it wouldn't be a complete meal.

What would a meat dish be without the right sauces or dressings or perhaps without the accompanying salad? Nothing!

In this book, you will find many recipes divided into five categories to enrich your dishes and enjoy every meal as a moment of full enjoyment!
You'll be able to combine them with other recipes you've received from friends and family or with recipes you may have already tried in other restaurants.

Do you want to organize a special lunch or dinner with family or friends? You could prepare several recipes in smaller portions, start the meal with soups and appetizers surrounded by creamy sauces and condiments, followed by several first and second courses, and finish it all off with fresh, crisp salads.

Imagine hearing the sound of water boiling in the background as you chop fresh, crisp vegetables. Smell the intense aroma of spices and herbs as you mix sauces and dressings. Imagine the joy of your guests as they prepare for a delicious meal you are cooking for them.

Imagine the explosion of your taste buds as you enjoy the final flavor of your creations, accentuated by the satisfaction of having cooked and created everything yourself.

PS.
When I first learned to cook, I would randomly jot down the changes I made to the ingredients next to the dishes. I fold the corners of the pages to find my favorite recipes faster. My cookbooks were not pretty to look that. While writing this book, I decided to include a space for notes next to each recipe. You'll find a tab at the end of the book where you can note which page your favorite recipes are on.

Benefits of Cooking at Home

Meals in the restaurant can contain several unhealthy ingredients. There is also much more than what you lack when you feed on a take-outs. These are some explanations of why you should consider having your cooking dinner tonight!

A Nutrient-Dense Plate

If prepared food arrives from outside the home, you typically have limited knowledge about salt, sugar, and processed oils. For a fact, we also apply more to our meal when it is served to the table. You will say how much salt, sugar, and oil are being used to prepare meals at home.

Increased Fruit and Vegetable Intake

The typical western diet loses both the weight and durability of plant foods we need to preserve. Many People eat only two fresh fruit and vegetables a day, while at least five portions are required. Tons of premade food, like restaurant food goods, restrict fruit and vegetable parts. By supplying you with the convenience of cooking at home, you have complete control over your food. The message to note is that your attention will continue with the intake of more fruit and vegetables. Attach them to your cooking, snack them, or exchange them with your relatives on their way. Then take steps towards organic alternatives. It is always better to eat entire fruits and vegetables, whether or not organic, than processed foods.

Save Money and Use What You Have

Just because you haven't visited your local health food or food store this week doesn't mean you get stuck with taking in. Open your cupboard and fridge and see what you can make for a meal. It can be as easy as gluten-free rice, roasted tomatoes, carrots, frozen vegetables, and lemon juice. This simple meal is packed with fiber, protein, vitamins, and minerals. Best of all, in less than 30 minutes, it is delicious and can be prepared. You can save up your money in the long run and allows you sufficient food to share with or break the next day.

Sensible Snacking

Bringing premade snacks saves time, but everything goes back to what's in these products still. Don't worry, you can still have your guilty pleasures, but there is a way to make them more nutritious and often taste better. Swap your chips and dip the chopped vegetables into hummus. Create your snacks with bagged potato chips or carrots. Take a bowl and make your popcorn on top of your stove or in the popcorn machine. You can manage the amount of salt, sugar, and oil added.

Share Your Delicious Health

Once you make your recipes, you are so proud of your achievements. Furthermore, the food tastes amazing. Don't confuse me now–some of your inventive recipes won't taste the same thing, but friends and family will love your cuisine with constant practice and experimentation. You will see them enjoy the best nutritious food because of you and your faith in spreading health and love.

It Gives You a Chance to Reconnect

Having that chance to cook together helps you reconnect with your partner and your loved ones. Cooking also has other benefits. The American Psychological Association says that working together with new things—like learning a new recipe—can help maintain a relationship.

It's Proven to Be Healthier

Many researchers say that those who eat more often than not have a healthier diet overall. Such studies also show that in restaurants, menus, salt, saturated fat, total fat, and average calories are typically higher than in-house diets.
You have complete control over your food, whether you put fresh products together or shipped them straight to your door using a company like Plated. It can make a difference in your overall health.

It's Easier to Watch Your Calories

The average fast-food order is between 1,100 and 1,200 calories in total–nearly all the highly recommended daily calorie intake is 1,600 to 2,400 calories by a woman and almost two thirds (2,000 to 3,000 calories) a man daily. So, think again if you felt the independent restaurants so smaller chains would do well. Such products suck up an average of 1.327 calories per meal of additional calories.

Adult BMI Calculation Formula

$$\text{BMI} = \frac{(\textbf{your weight} \text{ in pounds}) \times 703}{(\textbf{your height} \text{ in inches})^2}$$

FOR EXAMPLE:

If you weigh **120 pounds** and are **5 ft. 3in** (63in.) tall:

$$\text{BMI} = \frac{120 \times 703}{63^2} = \frac{84{,}360}{3{,}969} = 21.3$$

This is well within the healthy weight range

Creating your food ensures you can guarantee that the portion sizes and calories are where you want them. Recipes also come with nutritional information and tips for sizing, which ease this.

Body Mass Index Interpretation

BMI < 18.5:	Below normal weight
BMI >= 18.5 and < 25:	Normal weight
BMI >= 25 and < 30:	Overweight
BMI >= 30 and < 35:	Class I Obesity
BMI >= 35 and < 40:	Class II Obesity
BMI >= 40:	Class III Obesity

It's a Time Saver

Part of shopping is to wait for food to come or travel to get it. It may take much more time, depending on where you live, what time you order, and whether or not the delivery person is good at directions!
It doesn't have to take much time to cook at home if you don't want it. You remove the need to search for ingredients or foodstuffs by using a service like Plated. Everything you need is at your house, in the exact amount that you use.

It can be a money saver, too

In the long run, home-cooked food will save you money. A collection of basic ingredients also arrive at a lower price than a single dish. You can also consume more of a meal at home than if you buy a take-out or rest to work the next day. After a few weeks, you will see big savings starting to add up

It's Personalized

Cooking at home gives you the chance to enjoy the food you want, how you like it. For starters, with Plated, if you want your meat more well-done or less sweet, the formula includes suggested changes.

Cutting Costs

Nobody has to remind you that it's pricey to eat out. The disparity between a local restaurant sandwich and a kitchen sandwich is more than a feeling. The purchasing of packaged food in a restaurant typically costs far more than the buying of your
products. Cooking at home helps you get more for your money by raising the excess expenses of cooking and servicing restaurants. The more often you make your food, the more money you save.

Enjoying the Process

Once you come back home from a busy day, there is little more enjoyable than disconnecting from work emails, voicemails, unfinished assignments, or homework. Cooking at home presents you with a break from your routine and space for imagination. Rather than listen to noisy messages, you should put on the radio, collect spices, and reflect on the sizzle's odors on the stove or roast vegetables. It may stun you on how much you might like it when you make a daily habit of preparing food.

If your breakfast is great, lunch soup, or fresh tomato sauce for dinner, home cooking is a worthy investment. In return for your time and energy in preparation, you will benefit richly— from cost savings to fun with friends.

And the more you enjoy cooking in the kitchen, the more you get to make fantastic food!

Try Plated

Ready to download and cook your smartphone? Plated is a kind of a meal kit delivery service that offers all the above and more positive features!
Choose from a weekly menu of designed recipes and get all you need right at your door. Pre-portioned foods are of the highest quality only and contain fresh, seasonal, organically, and sustainable seafood items and hormone-free meat.
Recipes vary from meals that require just 30 minutes to prepare, which is as demanding as its rewards. Where people find dinner a delight to consume and cook.

Practical Advice for Beginners on the Correct Distribution of Meals During the Day, to Digest Well and Avoid Gaining Weight

Shifting to a healthy lifestyle seems to be intimidating. Being committed to your preferred diet, slowly and reasonably, will provide you lifelong changes and optimum health.

Start by selecting what seems doable to you. Follow your instincts when something piques your interest. You are the best at knowing what's right for you and what you will or will not eat or drink.

Be willing to trying something new because you will have to do something different, on purpose, if you want a different result. Don't worry about what you might give up. You don't have to decide to give up anything right now. Keep it easy. Once you go through the benefits of feeling better, having more energy, and looking better, it will be easier to embrace and maintain a healthy eating lifestyle.

The effortless mistake we've made by just only eating our food makes it a significant difference. It is vital to think that when it comes to our meals, timing is the key.

As for your breakfast, eating within 30 minutes of waking up is essential. 7 in the morning is the best time to have breakfast. Make sure to have your meal no later than 10 a.m. and always have protein in your breakfast.

Lastly, at 7 p.m., dinner is the perfect time to have your meal. It would be perfect for you to keep a 3 hours gap between dinner and bedtime. Have your meal before 10 p.m. because eating dinner close to bedtime might affect your good night's sleep.

One way to adapt a healthy eating lifestyle is to add vegetables and fruit to what you already eat gradually.

- At breakfast, include bananas, blueberries, blackberries, strawberries, or raspberries. Add spinach, onions, or bell peppers to eggs or egg whites.
- At lunch, have a cup of vegetable soup or a salad with your meal.
- At dinner, include an extra serving or two of vegetables.

In between meals, try having a piece of fruit such as orange, peach, apple or pear, or vegetables like celery, cucumber, carrots, tomatoes, or bell pepper. Meal dynamics is a way of saying that it's not just what you eat and when you eat that matters; how you eat matters, too! There are few variables in how one eats.

Your sequence: Main dish, salads, then dessert? How about having dessert first to guarantee that there is still room, instead of filling it all up? It is vital to deliberate on how customs lead us and to know whether it all makes sense. If you learn to yourself you want to have dessert, why not eat it first so you'll have time to relish it instead of stuffing it in when you're full?

Pace and duration: Are the meal more like a tweet or an essay? Is it more evocative of a furious choreography or ballroom dance? How long does it take to consume the meal?

Timing: If you have an AC eating schedule on your meals, do you eat your meal at the start of the eating window? Or at the end? Or do you nibble snack portion of foods through the window? Does it change anything if you eat carbohydrates first or last?

It can also be introduced that eating too heavy and too late promotes bad dreams, and the body focuses only on digestion and not on the regenerative processes of the body such as: skin renewal, treatment of infections and injuries of the body, hormones of satiety are not produced, the same as when you consume too much alcohol before going to bed.

Fast food may be adding to surplus fat in ways that go beyond being loaded with calories and engineered to have a compelling, appetite-stimulating taste and mouthfeel. Fast food is fast in another way: not only is it available quickly, but people tend to eat it and digest it promptly with complete absorption. The suitability of snacks such as burgers, smoothies, and fries help you achieve your calorie intake worth for a day in those 10 minutes of eating them. With all of those calories flowing down to your throat, you won't be able to measure your calorie intake from the first bite of your meal. You just paid for the meal, so you eat every edge to get the maximum value. It may not be ideal, because those extra bites expand your stomach, so it will allow you to eat more food later on to have that same feeling of fullness. Stomach stretch is a viral sensation that helps you know when you've had enough; it prevents you from spraining your stomach by savoring those extra bites. You get your superior value by having those different bites later, if not necessary, getting rid of those excess calories is still better than stuffing it into your body. Be mindful of ordering meals to avoid left-overs.

To use meal dynamics as a tool, you:

1. Eat low-calorie, high-volume foods first: Soups and salads are great for this for reasons mentioned in the "Meal Composition" section. Besides soups and salads, you can snack on pickles, cucumbers, celery, carrots, grape tomatoes, and other low-calorie foods with high water content instead of concentrated calorie juice, nuts, chips, or rapidly digested foods. Remember the Super-BCPs? (Sugars, pasta, rice, bread, cereal, and potatoes).

2. Nutrition experts say that you should focus on food by consciously sniffing and tasting so that your body can record the act of eating.

Take your time! Meals are not a pit stop where every second you reduce your eating time is an advantage for the daily rush.

Enjoy the aromas and the company of other people...

And if you have to eat alone, don't get tangled up in other activities at the same time. Do not chew or swallow hastily.
Bon appetite! If you take less than half an hour to eat, don't let your stomach and brain record everything you've eaten.
The dynamic of eating is to listen to your body and feel the natural feeling of satiety.
Even if you eat fast food, you can correct your appetite by eating it slowly.

Soup Recipes

Matsutake Clear Soup

Preparation Time: 15 minutes

Cooking Time: 20 minutes

Servings: 2

Ingredients:

- 4 stalks of Mitsuba
- 5.1 ounces of tofu (soft or silken), cut into small cubes
- 1 matsutake mushroom, cut into thin slices
- Yuzu zest
- 4 Temari Fu (optional)

For the dashi:

- 0.4 ounces of katsuobushi
- 0.2 ounces of kombu
- 2 cups of water

For seasoning:

- 2 teaspoons each of
- Soy sauce
- Mirin
- 1 tablespoon of sake
- Half a teaspoon of salt

Directions:

1. Use a damp towel to clean the matsutake mushrooms. Remember that you shouldn't wash them. Cut off and remove a thin slice of the stem of the mushroom, then cut into thin slices.
2. Clean the dashi kombu using a clean cloth. The white powdery substance increases the flavor of the umami in the dashi, so leave it on. Don't wash the dashi.
3. Take water in a medium-sized saucepan and add the kombu in it. Slowly heat in on medium-low heat. You can also dip it in water for up to half a day if you have time. Soaking it helps bring out the kombu's flavor naturally.

4. Add in the katsuobushi when it starts boiling. Allow it to simmer for thirty seconds and then turn off the heat. Line a sieve with a paper towel and keep it over a bowl. Strain the dashi into the bowl. Twist and squeeze the paper towel and release any excess dashi into the bowl.
5. Add the dashi into a saucepan and boil it. Add in the soy sauce, mirin, sake, and salt. Then, add in the tofu and the mushrooms and cook for two to three minutes. Add the Temari fu in water to allow it to hydrate. When it gets soft, squeeze out the water and transfer it into a serving bowl.
6. Take two Mitsuba stalks and tie them into a knot. Before serving, add the two knotted Mitsuba stalks into the soup.

Nutrition:

241 Calories, 21g Carbs, 4.1g Protein, 16g Fats

My notes:

Tofu and Japanese Pumpkin soup

Preparation Time: 15 minutes
Cooking Time: 45 minutes
Servings: 4

My notes:

Ingredients:

- 7 ounces of mixed mushrooms, trimmed and sliced
- 3 ounces of baby spinach
- 3.5 ounces of tofu (silken firm), cut into half-inch cubes
- 2 tablespoons of mirin
- 2-4 cup of soy sauce
- 2 sachets of instant dashi powder (0.7 ounces)
- 35 ounces of butternut pumpkin, peeled and cut into half-inch cubes
- Sesame seeds (toasted) and sesame oil, to serve

Directions:

1. Add six cups of slightly salted water into a saucepan placed over medium heat. Add in the pumpkin and simmer for ten to fifteen minutes so that they just soft. Add in the mirin, soy sauce, dashi powder, and tofu and let it simmer for five minutes. Mix in the mushrooms and spinach and cook for thirty seconds so that they wilt. Take it away from the heat. Transfer the soup into serving bowls and drizzle some sesame oil and top with toasted sesame seeds.

Nutrition:
145 Calories, 20g Carbs, 11g Protein, 3g Fats, 4g Fiber

Champon

My notes:

Preparation Time: 15 minutes

Cooking Time: 40 minutes

Servings: 2

Ingredients:

For preparing the soup:

- 2 cups of chicken broth
- 1 tablespoon each of
- Sake
- Soy sauce
- 1/4 cup of milk (whole)
- Half a teaspoon of salt
- 1 cup of dashi
- 1 teaspoon of sugar
- 1/8 teaspoon of pepper powder (white)

For preparing meat and the seafood:

- 2 ounces each of Pork belly (two slices) and Squid
- 11 teaspoon of soy sauce
- 2 and a half ounces of shrimp
- 1 tablespoon of sake

For the vegetables and other ingredients:

- 6 pieces of ear mushrooms (dried wood)
- 1/4 of an onion
- 1 ounce of snow pea
- 4 ounces of bean sprouts
- Black pepper (ground freshly)
- 11 ounces of Champon noodles
- 2 inches of carrot
- 5 ounces of cabbage
- A 1/3 of fish cake (kamaboko)
- 1 tablespoon of roasted sesame oil
- 1/8 teaspoon of salt

Directions:

1. Add the chicken broth (two cups) and the dashi (one cup) in a pot. Combine them with a spoon. To this mixture, add soy sauce, sake, and granulated sugar (one teaspoon). Allow them to cook.
2. Once they start boiling, add the milk and white pepper. Slice the pork belly into pieces of one inch. Add soy sauce and sake (each of one teaspoon) to it. Place the shrimp, squid, and two teaspoons of sake in the bowl. Set aside for about five minutes.
3. Slice the squid by moving the knife diagonally (make parallel lines). You can make simple incisions on the flesh.
4. Take another bowl and add then the mushrooms. Pour enough water in the bowl to immerse the mushroom pieces. Rehydrate the mushrooms to soften them and then squeeze out the extra water. Slice into pieces.
5. Make thin slabs of the carrot and then half the slices vertically. Chop the onion. Discarding the core of cabbage, cut them into cubes. Cut the snow peas into halves after removing the strings from them. Make thin slices of the kamaboko fish.
6. Place a wok over moderate to high heat and add sesame oil to it. After the oil starts to boil, add pork belly pieces and cook until they brown. Add the squid and the shrimp pieces to it and cook until they become opaque.
7. Stir in carrot and onion. Add mushroom and cabbage, and keep stirring for one minute. Stir in the bean sprouts, the snow peas, and fish—Cook for an additional minute. Sprinkle pepper and then toss them to combine. Add the soup to the wok and then adjust the salt by tasting it.
8. Prepare the noodles: Cut the packet, take the noodles out, and then separate them, place a large pan over a moderate flame, and pour water. Put the noodle strips in it—Cook noodles and place in a bowl. Top the noodles with the soup and other toppings. Serve them warm.

Nutrition:

522 Calories, 93g Carbs, 23g Protein, 18g Fats

Soba Noodles with Sake-Poached Chicken

Preparation Time: 15 minutes

Cooking Time: 50 minutes

Servings: 4

Ingredients:

- 1/4 each cup of Shiitake mushrooms and Light soy sauce
- Half a cup of sake
- 2 cups of chicken stock
- 1.5 tsps. of caster sugar
- 2 chicken breasts (6.5 oz. each)
- A bunch of Bok choy
- 2 cups of enoki mushrooms
- 1 red chili (long, sliced thinly)
- 1 packed of soba noodles (9.5 ounces)

Directions:

1. Add two cups of hot water to shiitake mushrooms in a bowl. Keep them aside for five minutes and then drain them. The mushroom liquid should be reserved.
2. Now, in a saucepan, add the following ingredients – reserved mushroom liquid, chicken stock, sugar, soy sauce, and sake. Simmer on medium flame and keep stirring.
3. Then, add the chicken and keep cooking for another ten minutes. Flip the pieces of chicken and then add the bok choy—Cook for about eight minutes. Pour the bok choy and chicken to a plate.

4. Simmer the broth again. Add the shiitake mushrooms, enoki mushrooms, and the noodles. Cook them for about eight minutes. Now, divide into bowls for serving. On top of the noodles, add shredded chicken, bok choy, mushrooms, and sliced red chili. Then, use a spoon to divide the broth into the bowls.

Nutrition:
452 Calories, 57.8g Carbs, 41.9g Protein, 4.2g Fats, 1g Fiber

My notes:

Soba Noodles with Miso Salmon

Preparation Time: 15 minutes

Cooking Time: 15 minutes

Servings: 4

Ingredients:

- 2 bunches of broccolini
  (cut into halves lengthwise after trimming)
- 1 tablespoon of mirin
- 1.5 tablespoons of white miso paste
- 1 packet of soba noodles (8 oz.)
- 2 teaspoons of sake
- 1 teaspoon each of sesame oil and of caster sugar
- 17.5 oz. of salmon fillets (boned and skinned)
- 1 cup of red cabbage (sliced thinly)
- 3 cups of mesclun leaves
- For serving - mixed sesame seeds

For the ponzu dressing:

- 1/4 cup of soy sauce
- Juice of half a lemon
- 1 tablespoon each of mirin and sake

Directions:

1. In a large-sized saucepan, boil water and add some salt in it—Cook the soba noodles. Add the broccolini in the noodles just two minutes before completion. Drain and keep the noodles aside. Set your grill on high. In a small-sized bowl, combine mirin, miso, sugar, sake, and sesame oil.
2. Take a baking tray and use foil to line the tray. Place the fillets of salmon on the tray. Take the miso mixture and brush it on the fillets. Grill the salmon for about five minutes, and they should become lightly charred. Keep them aside for five minutes. Flake them roughly.

3. Now, take a large-sized bowl and combine the dressing along with the noodles and broccolini. Add the mesclun leaves too. Toss everything well and divide into serving bowls. Top with sesame seeds and grilled salmon before serving.

Nutrition:

413 Calories, 31g Carbs, 13g Protein, 25g Fats

My notes:

Appetizer Recipes

Olive Garden Tomato Basil Crostini

Preparation Time: 10 minutes

Cooking Time: 10 minutes

Servings: 4

Ingredients:

- 4 chopped medium tomatoes
- 6–8 chopped fresh basil leaves
- 6 tablespoons extra-virgin olive oil
- 8 slices of crusty bread
- 2–3 cloves of garlic

Directions:

1. In a medium bowl, mix the tomatoes, basil, and olive oil together. Grill or toast the bread. Rub the bread with garlic and top with the tomato mixture.

Nutrition:

269 Calories, 15g Fats, 10g Protein

My notes:

Chili's Chicken Fajita Nachos

Preparation Time: 15 minutes

Cooking Time: 10 minutes

Servings: 2

My notes:

Ingredients:

- 1 chicken breast strips
- 1 sliced Vidalia onion
- 1 bell pepper, cut into thin strips
- 1 envelope fajita seasoning mix
- 16 large tortilla chips
- ½ cup shredded Cheddar cheese
- ½ cup shredded Monterey jack cheese
- 16 jarred jalapeño pepper slices
- 1 cup shredded lettuce
- ½ cup thick and chunky salsa
- 2 tablespoons sour cream
- 2 tablespoons guacamole

Directions:

1. Sauté chicken, onions, and bell peppers following the fajita seasoning packet. Drain and set aside. Put tortilla chips on a large plate, then layer the cooked chicken fajita on top. Put some cheese and jalapeno on top, then microwave for 3 minutes. Lastly, garnish it with lettuce, salsa, sour cream, and guacamole.

Nutrition:

279 Calories, 18.1g Fats, 12.4g Protein

Panda Express's Veggie Spring Roll

Preparation Time: 15 minutes

Cooking Time: 5 minutes

Servings: 6-8

Ingredients:

- 4 teaspoons vegetable oil, divided
- 3 eggs, beaten
- 1 medium head cabbage, finely shredded
- ½ carrot, julienned
- 1 (8-ounce) can shredded bamboo shoots
- 1 cup dried, shredded wood ear mushroom, rehydrated
- 1-pound Chinese barbecue or roasted pork, cut into matchsticks
- ½ cup chopped Chinese yellow chives
- 1 green onion, thinly sliced
- 2½ teaspoons soy sauce
- 1 teaspoon salt
- 1 teaspoon sugar
- 1 (14-ounce) package egg roll wrappers
- 1 egg white, beaten
- 1-quart oil for frying, or as needed

Directions:

1. In a large skillet, heat 1 tablespoon of oil over medium-high heat.
2. When the skillet is hot, add the beaten eggs and cook until firm, then flip and cook a bit longer like an omelet. When set, remove from the pan. Cut into strips and set aside.
3. Add the remaining oil to the skillet and heat. When hot, add the cabbage and carrot and cook for a couple of minutes until they start to soften. Then add the bamboo shoots, mushrooms, pork, green onions, chives, soy sauce, salt, and sugar. Cook until the veggies are soft, then stir in the egg. Transfer the mixture to a bowl and refrigerate for about 1 hour.

4. When cooled, add about 2–3 tablespoons of filling to each egg roll wrapper. Brush some beaten egg around the edges of the wrapper and roll up, tucking in the ends first.
5. When all the wrappers are filled, heat about 6 inches of oil to 350°F in a deep saucepan, Dutch oven or fryer.
6. Add the egg rolls to the hot oil a couple at a time. When golden brown and crispy, remove from oil to a paper-towel-lined plate to drain.
7. Serve with chili sauce or sweet and sour sauce.

Nutrition:

132 Calories, 3.3g Fats, 5.5g Carbs, 32g Protein

My notes:

PF Chang's Lettuce Wraps

Preparation Time: 10 minutes
Cooking Time: 10 minutes
Servings: 4

My notes:

Ingredients:

- 1 tablespoon olive oil
- 1-pound ground chicken
- 2 cloves garlic, minced
- 1 onion, diced
- ¼ cup hoisin sauce
- 2 tablespoons soy sauce
- 1 tablespoon rice wine vinegar
- 1 tablespoon ginger, freshly grated
- 1 tablespoon Sriracha (optional)
- 1 (8-ounce) can whole water chestnuts, drained and diced
- 2 green onions, thinly sliced
- Kosher salt and freshly ground black pepper to taste
- 1 head iceberg lettuce

Directions:

1. Add the oil to a deep skillet or saucepan and heat over medium-high heat. When hot, add the chicken and cook until it is completely cooked through. Stir while cooking to make sure it is properly crumbled.
2. Drain any excess fat from the skillet, then add the garlic, onion, hoisin sauce, soy sauce, ginger, sriracha, and vinegar. Cook until the onions have softened, then stir in the water chestnuts and green onion and cook for another minute or so. Add salt and pepper to taste.
3. Serve with lettuce leaves and eat by wrapping them up like a taco.

Nutrition:

156 Calories, 4.3g Fats, 3.7g Carbs, 27g Protein

Pei Wei's Vietnamese Chicken Salad Spring Roll

Preparation Time: 10 minutes

Cooking Time: 1 minute

Servings: 4-6

Ingredients:

Salad:

Rice Wrappers:

- Green leaf lettuce like Boston Bibb lettuce
- Napa cabbage, shredded
- Green onions, chopped
- Mint, chopped
- Carrots, cut into 1-inch matchsticks
- Peanuts

Lime dressing:

- 2 tablespoons lime juice, about 1 lime
- 1½ teaspoons water
- 1 tablespoon sugar
- 1 teaspoon salt
- Dash of pepper
- 3 tablespoons oil
- Peanut dipping sauce:
- 2 tablespoons soy sauce
- 1 tablespoon rice wine vinegar
- 2 tablespoons brown sugar
- ¼ cup peanut butter
- 1 teaspoon chipotle Tabasco
- 1 teaspoon honey
- 1 teaspoon sweet chili sauce
- 1 teaspoon lime vinaigrette

Directions:

Lime dressing:

1. Add everything but the oil to a small container or bowl and shake or stir until the sugar and salt are dissolved. Next, add the oil and shake well.

Peanut Dipping Sauce:

2. Add all the ingredients to a small bowl and mix to combine thoroughly.

Assembling:

3. In a large bowl, mix together all the salad ingredients except for the rice wrappers and lettuce.
4. Place the rice wrappers in warm water for about 1 minute to soften.
5. Transfer the wrappers to a plate and top each with 2 pieces of lettuce.
6. Top the lettuce with the salad mixture and drizzle with the lime dressing. Fold the wrapper by tucking in the ends and then rolling.
7. Serve with lime dressing and peanut dipping sauce.

Nutrition:

178 Calories, 4.4g Fats, 7g Carbs, 68g Protein

My notes:

Outback Steakhouse Bloomin' Onion

Preparation Time: 10 minutes

Cooking Time: 5 minutes

Servings: 4

Ingredients:

Seasoned Flour:

- 2 cups flour
- 4 teaspoons paprika
- 2 teaspoons garlic powder
- ½ teaspoon pepper
- ¼ teaspoon cayenne pepper

Batter:

- 1/3 cup cornstarch
- 1½ cups flour
- 2 teaspoons minced garlic
- 2 teaspoons paprika
- 1 teaspoon salt
- 1 teaspoon pepper
- 24 ounces beer
- 1 Vidalia or Texas sweet onion

Directions:

1. Preheat oil in a deep fryer to 375°F. In a shallow bowl, combine all seasoned flour ingredients. Prepare the batter: mix cornstarch, flour, and seasonings until well blended. Add the beer and mix well.
2. Cut about ¾″ on top of onion and peel. Cut 12–16 vertical wedges, but do not cut through the bottom root end. Remove about 1″ of petals from the center of the onion.
3. Dip prepared onion in seasoned flour and remove the excess by shaking. Separate the petals and dip into the batter to coat thoroughly.

4. Gently place in the fryer basket and deep-fry 1½ minutes. Turn the onion over and fry an additional 1½ minutes. Drain on paper towels. Place onion upright in a shallow bowl and remove center core with a circular cutter or apple corer.

Nutrition:

280 Calories, 16g Fats, 11g Protein

My notes:

T.G.I. Friday's Baked Potato Skins

Preparation Time: 10 minutes

Cooking Time: 15 minutes

Servings: 5

Ingredients:

- 10 baked potato halves
- 1 tablespoon melted butter
- Seasoned salt, to taste
- ¾ cup shredded Cheddar cheese
- 5 strips of cooked and crumbled bacon
- 1 green onion, diced

Directions:

1. Preheat oven to 375°F. Remove as much of the potato flesh as you can, leaving only the skins. Brush potato shells with butter and season with salt. Bake for 15–20 minutes, until crisp. Remove and sprinkle with cheese, bacon, and onion. Place back in the oven for 6–8 minutes until the cheese has melted. Serve with sour cream or ranch dressing.

Nutrition:

281 Calories, 15g Fats, 11g Protein

My notes:

Takeout Dry Garlic Ribs

Preparation Time: 15 minutes

Cooking Time: 2 hours and 15 minutes

Servings: 4-6

My notes:

Ingredients:

- 6 pounds pork ribs
- 1½ cups broth
- 1½ cups brown sugar
- ¼ cup soy sauce
- 12 cloves garlic, minced
- ¼ cup yellow mustard
- 1 large onion, finely chopped
- ¼ teaspoon salt
- ½ teaspoon black pepper

Directions:

1. Preheat oven to 200 degrees. Season ribs with salt and pepper and place on a baking tray. Cover with aluminum foil and bake for 1 hour.
2. In a mixing bowl, stir together the broth, brown sugar, soy sauce, garlic, mustard, and onion. Continue stirring until the sugar is completely dissolved. After an hour, remove the foil from the ribs and turn the heat up to 350°F.
3. Carefully pour the sauce over the ribs. Re-cover with the foil and return to the oven for 1 hour. Remove the foil and bake for 15 more minutes on each side.

Nutrition:

233 Calories, 3.6g Fats, 6.4g Carbs, 65g Protein

Abuelo's Jalapeno Poppers

Preparation Time: 10 minutes

Cooking Time: 1 hour and 10 minutes

Servings: 8

Ingredients:

- 30 jalapeno peppers
- 1 cup milk
- 2 packages soften cream cheese, at room temperature (8-ounces each)
- 1/8 teaspoon paprika
- 12 ounces Cheddar cheese, shredded
- 1/8 teaspoon chili powder
- 1 cup flour
- 1/8 teaspoon garlic powder
- 1 cup seasoned breadcrumbs
- ¼ teaspoon ground black pepper
- 1 quart of oil for frying
- ¼ teaspoon salt

Directions:

1. Scrape out seeds and the pith inside of the jalapeno peppers using a spoon. Combine cheddar cheese together with cream cheese in a medium-sized bowl; give them a good stir until blended well. Fill each pepper half with the prepared cream cheese blend using a spoon.
2. Add flour into a small-sized shallow bowl. Add paprika, pepper, garlic powder, chili powder, and salt. Blend into the flour until it is mixed. Pour milk into a separate medium-sized shallow bowl. Dip stuffed jalapeno into flour. Place the floured pepper on a large-sized baking sheet with a rack. Let dry for 10 minutes.
3. Pour the dried breadcrumbs into a separate bowl. Dip the floured jalapeno pepper into the milk & then into the bowl with the breadcrumbs. Place the pepper on the rack again. Preheat the oil to

350 F in advance. Dip pepper into the milk & then into the breadcrumbs. Repeat these steps until you have utilized the entire dipping peppers.

4. Work in batches and fry peppers for a minute or two, until turn golden brown. Remove from oil & place them on a baking rack to drain.

Nutrition:

257 Calories, 14.3g Fats, 18.9g Carbs, 21.5g Protein

My notes:

Applebee's Baja Potato Boats

Preparation Time:10 minutes

Cooking Time: 30 minutes

Servings: 4

Ingredients:

For Pico de Gallo:

- 1 ½ teaspoon fresh cilantro, minced
- 1 tablespoon canned jalapeño slices (nacho slices), diced
- 3 tablespoons Spanish onion, chopped
- 1 chopped tomato (approximately ½ cup)
- A dash each of freshly-ground black pepper & salt

For the Potato Boats:

- 2 slices Canadian bacon diced (roughly 2 tablespoons)
- Canola oil nonstick cooking spray, as required
- ⅓ cup Cheddar cheese, shredded - 3 russet potatoes, medium
- ⅓ cup Mozzarella cheese - salt as needed
- On the Side: - Salsa & sour cream

Directions:

1. Combine the entire Pico De Gallo ingredients together in a large bowl; mix well. When done, place in a refrigerator until ready to use.
2. Preheat your oven to 400 F in advance. Place potatoes in oven & bake until tender, for an hour. Set aside at room temperature until easy to handle. When done, cut them lengthwise 2 times. This should make 3 ½ to ¾" slices, throwing the middle slices away.
3. Increase your oven's temperature to 450 F. Take a spoon & scoop out the inside of the potato skins. Ensure that you must leave at least ¼ of an inch of the potato inside each skin. Spray the potato skin completely on all sides with the spray of nonstick canola oil. Put the skins, cut-side facing up on a large-sized cookie sheet. Sprinkle them with salt & bake in the preheated oven until the edges start to turn brown, for 12 to 15 minutes.

4. Combine both the cheeses together in a large bowl. Sprinkle approximately 1 ½ tablespoon of the mixture on each potato skin. Then sprinkle a teaspoon of the Canadian bacon over the cheese. Top this with a large tablespoon of the Pico de Gallo and then sprinkle each skin with some more cheese.
5. Place the skins into the oven again & bake until the cheese melts, for 2 to 4 more minutes. Remove & let them sit for a minute. Slice each one lengthwise using a sharp knife. Serve hot with some salsa and sour cream on the side.

Nutrition:

254 Calories, 24g Fats, 43g Carbs, 55g Protein

My notes:

Chicken Lettuce Wraps

Preparation Time: 5 minutes

Cooking Time: 25 minutes

Servings: 2

Ingredients:

- 2 chicken breasts, boneless skinless
- 2/3 cup mushroom
- 4 -5 leaves of iceberg lettuce
- 1 teaspoon garlic, minced
- 3 tablespoons onions, chopped
- 1 cup water chestnut
- 3 tablespoons oil

For Stir Fry Sauce:

- 2 tablespoons brown sugar
- ½ teaspoon rice wine vinegar
- 2 tablespoons soy sauce

For Special Sauce:

- 2 tablespoons rice wine vinegar
- 1 -2 teaspoon red chili & garlic paste
- ¼ cup sugar
- 1 tablespoon lemon juice
- 2 tablespoons soy sauce
- 1 tablespoon hot mustard
- 2 tablespoons ketchup
- 1/8 teaspoon sesame oil
- ½ cup plus 2 teaspoons water

Directions:

1. Dissolve sugar with water in a small sized bowl. Add in the rice wine vinegar, soy sauce, ketchup, sesame oil & lemon juice; mix well & prepare the special sauce; cover & let refrigerate until ready to serve.

2. Now, combine hot mustard with hot water; set aside. To pour over the wraps, add in the garlic chili & mustard sauce in the end to the special sauce mixture.
3. Over high heat in a large frying pan or wok; heat the oil & sauté the chicken breasts until done, for 4 to 5 minutes on each side. Remove the chicken pieces from the heat & let cool at room temperature for a couple of minutes.
4. Don't remove the oil; keep it in the pan & try to keep it hot. In the meantime, mince the mushrooms and water chestnuts to the size of small peas.
5. Now, make the stir fry sauce: In a small bowl, mix soy sauce together with rice vinegar & brown sugar; mix well. When you can handle the chicken easily and once cool, mince it as the water chestnuts and mushrooms are. Add a tablespoon of vegetable oil more to the pan & add in the garlic, chicken, onions, mushrooms & water chestnuts to the hot pan. Add in the stir fry sauce, sauté the mixture for a couple of minutes, then serve in the lettuce leaves.

Nutrition:

287 Calories, 6.9g Carbs, 59g Protein

My notes:

Old and Modern Sauce and Dressing Recipes

Lipton Onion Soup Mix

Preparation Time: 5 minutes

Cooking Time: 0 minutes

Servings: 4

Ingredients:

- 1½ cups dry onion flakes
- ½ cup beef bouillon powder
- 8 teaspoons onion powder
- ½ teaspoon crushed celery seeds
- ½ teaspoon dry parsley
- ½ teaspoon sugar

Directions:

1. Combine all ingredients in a jar. Store it with an airtight cover.

Nutrition:

19 Calories, 0.4g Fats, 4.2g Carbs

My notes:

Heinz Ketchup

Preparation Time: 25 minutes

Cooking Time: 20 minutes

Servings: 4

Ingredients:

- 1 cup tomato paste
- ⅓ cup light corn syrup
- ½ cup white vinegar
- ⅓ cup water
- 2 tablespoons sugar
- Salt, to taste
- ⅓ teaspoon onion powder
- ¼ teaspoon garlic powder

Directions:

1. Combine all the ingredients in a saucepan. Turn on the heat and let the liquid simmer for 20 minutes. Turn off the heat and let the mixture cool down. Store it in an airtight glass jar or serve with French fries.

Nutrition:

78 Calories, 0.2g Fats, 19.3g Carbs, 1.4g Protein

My notes:

Caramel Sauce

My notes:

Preparation Time: 8 minutes

Cooking Time: 8 minutes

Servings: 12

Ingredients:

- 1 ½ cups of brown sugar
- 4 tbsps. of all-purpose flour
- 1 cup of boiling water
- a pinch of salt (½ tsp)
- 2 tbsps. of butter
- 2 tbsps. of heavy cream
- vanilla (optional, to taste)

Directions:

1. Heat a pan over medium-high heat and mix together the flour and sugar, stirring well.
2. Once the contents have mixed well, stir in the water & salt. Allow to cook for 6 minutes, stirring regularly so that the sugar is well blended. If the mix gets too thick, slowly mix more water in.
3. Remove from heat and mix in the butter, cream, and vanilla. Stir well to mix and melt all the ingredients together.

Nutrition:

123 Calories, 24g Carbs, 3g Fats, 1g Protein

Chili's Original Chili

Preparation Time: 15 minutes

Cooking Time: 1 hour 30 minutes

Servings: 4

Ingredients:

Spice Blend:

- ½ cup chili powder
- ⅛ cup salt
- ⅛ cup ground cumin
- 1 tablespoon paprika
- 1 teaspoon ground black pepper
- 1 teaspoon garlic powder
- 1 teaspoon of cayenne pepper

Chili:

- 4 pounds chuck, ground for chili
- 3¼ cups water
- 16 ounces tomato sauce
- 1½ cups yellow onions, chopped
- 1 tablespoon cooking oil

Masa Harina:

- 1 cup water
- 1 tablespoon Masa Harina
- Sliced green onions for garnish, if desired

Directions:

1. Put all the spice blend ingredients in a bowl. Mix thoroughly and set the bowl aside. Cook the meat over medium heat in a stockpot until it is brown. While the meat is cooking, thoroughly mix together the spice mix, water, and tomato sauce.
2. Add the spice mixture to the browned meat and bring to a boil. When the chili is about to boil, sauté the onions in oil over medium heat for the meantime. When the chili is boiling, and the onions are translucent, add the onions to the chili and stir.

3. Adjust the heat to low and let the chili simmer for an hour, stirring the mixture every 15 minutes. In a bowl, mix the Masa Harina ingredients together. When the chili has been cooking for an hour, add the Masa Harina mixture to the chili and cook for another 10 minutes.
4. Transfer the chili to a bowl, garnish green onions, if desired, and serve.

Nutrition:
681 Calories, 48g Fats, 32g Protein

My notes:

Duck Sauce

My notes:

Preparation Time: 5 minutes

Cooking Time: 2 minutes

Servings: 4

Ingredients:

- 2 teaspoons sugar
- 1 ½ tbsps. of hot water
- 3 tbsps. of apricot preservatives
- 1 salted pickled plum (pitted)
- ½ a tsp of juice from pickled plum
- ⅛ tsp of soy sauce
- ¼ tsp of rice vinegar

Directions:

1. Stir the sugar and hot water together in a bowl, until the sugar is dissolved. Add the apricot preserves and plum into the bowl and stir with a fork to break up the contents.
2. Pour in the remaining ingredients: juice from the pickled plum, soy sauce, and vinegar. Stir well and then leave the sauce to sit for 5 minutes. Stir one last time and then serve. You can store duck sauce for several months.

Nutrition:

53 Calories, 14g Carbs, 1g Fat, 1g Protein

Chipotle's Guacamole

Preparation Time: 10 minutes

Cooking Time: 0 minutes

Servings: 6

Ingredients:

- 1 medium jalapeño pepper, seeded and deveined, finely chopped
- 1 cup diced red onion
- 2 tablespoons fresh cilantro, chopped finely
- 8 ripe avocados
- 8 teaspoons freshly squeezed lime juice
- 1 teaspoon kosher salt

Directions:

1. Chop avocado in half and take out the flesh. Mix in the jalapeño pepper, onion, and cilantro. Drizzle the lime juice. Season it with salt. Pound avocado with the rest of the ingredients until desired consistency is achieved. Seal it with plastic wrap before serving.

Nutrition:

674 Calories, 37g Fats, 26g Protein

My notes:

Café Rio's Pico de Gallo

Preparation Time: 5 minutes

Cooking Time: 0 minutes

Servings: 6

Ingredients:

- 5 ripe tomatoes, finely diced
- ½ teaspoon salt
- 1 medium sweet onion, finely diced
- 4 cloves garlic, minced
- 1 bunch cilantro, finely chopped
- 1–2 jalapeño peppers, seeded and diced
- 1 tablespoon lime juice
- 4 shakes green Tabasco sauce

Directions:

1. Mix all the ingredients. Serve at room temperature.

Nutrition:

664 Calories, 48g Fats, 29g Protein

My notes:

Newman Own's Creamy Caesar Salad Dressing

Preparation Time: 5 minutes

Cooking Time: 0 minutes

Servings: 10

Ingredients:

- 2 cups mayonnaise
- 6 tablespoons white vinegar, distilled
- ¼ cup Parmesan cheese, grated
- 4 teaspoons Worcestershire sauce
- 1 teaspoon lime juice
- 1 teaspoon dry mustard, ground
- ⅓ teaspoon salt, or to taste
- ½ teaspoon garlic powder
- ½ teaspoon onion powder
- ½ teaspoon black pepper, freshly ground
- 1 pinch basil, dried
- 1 pinch oregano, dried

Directions:

1. Take an electric mixer and blend all the ingredients until smooth. Chill the prepared dressing for a few hours before severing. Enjoy.

Nutrition:

215 Calories, 17.4g Fats,

13.3g Carbs, 2.3g Protein

Lawry's Seasoned Salt

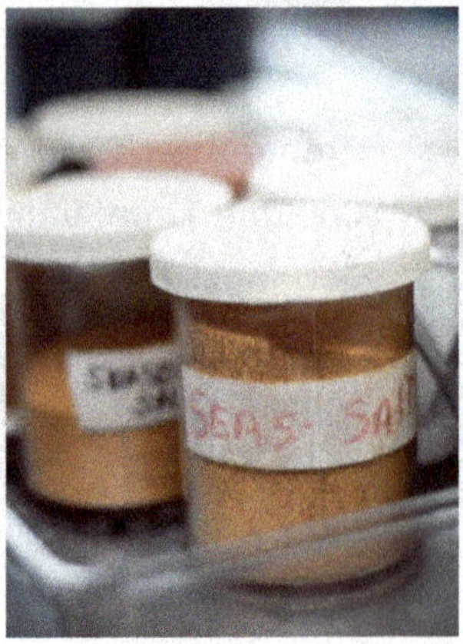

Preparation Time: 5 minutes

Cooking Time: 0 minutes

Servings: 1

Ingredients:

- 1 tablespoon salt, or to taste
- 2 teaspoons white sugar
- ¼ teaspoon smoked paprika
- ¼ teaspoon turmeric powder
- ¼ teaspoon onion powder
- ¼ teaspoon garlic powder
- ¼ teaspoon cornstarch

Directions:

1. Combine all the spices in a bowl and store in a glass jar. Keep it dry.

Nutrition:

360mg Sodium

My notes:

Pollo Tropical's Curry Mustard Sauce

Preparation Time: 5 minutes

Cooking Time: 0 minutes

Servings: 12

Ingredients:

- 2 teaspoon curry powder
- 4 teaspoons mustard paste
- 8 tablespoons mayonnaise

Directions:

1. Plug in a food processor, add all the ingredients in it, cover with the lid and then pulse for 30 seconds until smooth.
2. Tip the sauce into a bowl and then serve.

Nutrition:

66 Calories, 7 g Fats, 1 g Protein

My notes:

Sweet Chili Sauce

Preparation Time: 5 minutes

Cooking Time: 15 minutes

Servings: 6

Ingredients:

- 1 tablespoon garlic chili sauce
- ½ cup of water
- 2 scoops of beef bone broth collagen
- ¼ cup unseasoned rice vinegar
- 1 ½ teaspoon minced garlic
- ¼ teaspoon ground ginger
- ¼ cup erythritol sweetener
- 1 tablespoon avocado oil

Directions:

1. Take a large bowl, place all the ingredients in it except for oil and then whisk well until well combined.
2. Take a medium saucepan, place it over medium heat, add sauce mixture, and then simmer it for 15 minutes until the sauce has thickened.
3. When done, remove the pan from heat, stir in oil, let the sauce cool completely and then serve.

Nutrition:

25 Calories, 2.2 g Fats, 1.2 g Net Carb

My notes:

Chorizo Queso Fundido

Preparation Time: 5 minutes

Cooking Time: 25 minutes

Servings: 6

Ingredients:

- 8 ounces Mexican chorizo
- 1 Roma tomato, cored, seeded, and diced
- 2 tablespoons minced garlic
- 1/2 of a large onion, peeled, sliced
- 1 roasted poblano pepper, seeded, cut into strips
- ½ teaspoon of sea salt
- 2 cups shredded Monterey Jack Cheese
- 1 cup Mexican cream

Directions:

1. Take a large skillet pan, place it over medium heat, add chorizo, break it up and then cook for 10 to 12 minutes until nicely brown and crisp.
2. When done, drain excess grease, transfer chorizo to a bowl, and then set it aside until required.
3. Return pan over medium heat, add onion and then cook it for 5 minutes until tender.
4. Add tomato, pepper strips, and garlic, season with salt, cook the mixture for 2 minutes until hot and then spoon the mixture into the bowl containing chorizo.
5. Remove skillet pan from the heat, pour in cream and cheese, and then blend for 5 minutes or more until cheese has melted.
6. Return the skillet pan over medium heat, add half of the chorizo mixture, stir until mixed and cook for 5 minutes until creamy.

7. Top it with the remaining chorizo mixture, place the pan under the broiler and cook for 3 minutes until the mixture begins to bubble.
8. Serve it with low-carb tortilla chips.

Nutrition:

402 Calories, 33 g Fats, 22 g Protein, 4 g Net Carb, 1 g Fiber

My notes:

Old and Modern Lunch and Dinner Recipes

Chicken Carbonara

Preparation Time: 20 minutes

Cooking Time: 30 minutes

Servings: 4

Ingredients:

- Marinated chicken or shrimp
- 1 cup extra-virgin olive oil
- 1 cup hot water
- 1 tablespoon Italian seasoning
- 1 tablespoon chopped garlic
- 3 pounds chicken strips or large shrimp, peeled and deveined

Sauce:

- 1 cup butter
- 1½ teaspoons garlic, chopped
- 3 tablespoons bacon bits
- 3 tablespoons all-purpose flour
- 1 cup parmesan cheese, grated
- 1-quart heavy cream
- 1-quart milk
- ¼ cup bacon base
- ½ teaspoon black pepper
- 1¾ pounds long pasta (spaghetti, linguine, etc.) cooked according to package **Directions**
- ¼ teaspoon salt

Topping:

- 3 tablespoons Romano cheese, grated
- 3 tablespoons parmesan cheese, grated
- 1¾ cups mozzarella cheese, shredded
- ½ cup panko breadcrumbs
- 1½ teaspoons garlic, chopped
- 1½ tablespoons butter, melted
- 2 tablespoons parsley, chopped
- Marinated chicken strips (or shrimp) as above

- 1½ cups roasted red peppers, cut into small strips
- ¼ cup bacon bits

Directions:

1. Preheat oven to 350°F. In a mixing bowl, whisk together olive oil with hot water, Italian seasoning, and chopped garlic. Let chicken/shrimp marinate for at least 30 minutes in the refrigerator.
2. To make the sauce, melt the butter over medium heat in a large saucepan. Sauté the garlic and bacon bits for 5 minutes, stirring frequently.
3. Add the flour, parmesan cheese, heavy cream, milk, bacon base, pepper, and salt. Whisk well. Bring to a boil, then reduce heat and allow to simmer.
4. To make the topping, mix the romano cheese, parmesan, mozzarella cheese, panko, chopped garlic, melted butter, and chopped parsley in a mixing bowl. Blend well. Set aside.
5. Heat a large skillet to cook the chicken and/or shrimp. Add the red peppers and bacon bits. Cook for 3 minutes or until meat is cooked through. Add sauce and stir.
6. Add pasta. Mix well to coat the pasta evenly. Top with extra cheese, if desired. Serve.

Nutrition:

510 Calories, 6.3g Carbs, 30g Protein

My notes:

Texas Road House's Mesquite Grilled Pork Chops with Cinnamon Apples

Preparation Time: 40 minutes

Cooking Time: 40 minutes

Servings: 2

Ingredients:

Cinnamon Apples:

- 4 apples (peeled, sliced)
- 2 tablespoons butter, melted
- ⅓ cup brown sugar
- 2 tablespoons lemon juice
- ¾ teaspoon cinnamon

Pork Chop:

- 2 pork loin chops with bone, room temperature; 2 inches thick

Paste:

- 2 tablespoons extra virgin olive oil
- 2 tablespoons Worcestershire sauce
- 2 teaspoons black pepper, cracked
- 2 teaspoons chili powder
- 2 teaspoons granulated garlic powder
- 2 teaspoons kosher salt
- 1 teaspoon cumin, ground
- ½ teaspoon cinnamon, ground
- Mesquite wood chips, soaked in water for at least 30 minutes

Directions:

1. Prepare the apples by cooking all the cinnamon apple ingredients in butter until the apples soften. When they are ready, set the cooked apples aside. Reheat before serving.
2. Before you begin with the meat, you need to:
3. Soak the mesquite chips as instructed; Leave the pork loin at room temperature for 30 to 45 minutes; and Preheat the grill on high.

4. Thoroughly mix all the paste ingredients together. When the paste is done, spread it over the pork chops, covering them completely. Remove the chips from the water and place them in an aluminum foil pan.
5. Place the pan directly over the fire from the grill and cook the pork loin on both sides for about 6 minutes. When the meat is seared, lower the heat to medium. Place the pork over indirect medium heat and cook for another 25 minutes. Remove the pork from heat, wrap it in aluminum foil, and let rest for another 5 minutes. Transfer the pork to a plate with the reheated apples. Serve the entire dish.

Nutrition:

316 Calories, 22.5g Fats, 9.1g Carbs, 20.5g Protein

My notes:

Panda Express's Sweet Fire Chicken Breast

Preparation Time: 15 minutes
Cooking Time: 15 minutes
Servings: 4

Ingredients:

- 3 large chicken breasts, cut into 1-inch pieces
- 1 (10-ounce) bottle sweet chili sauce
- 1 medium onion, sliced
- 1 large red bell pepper, chopped
- 1¼ cup pineapple chunks
- ¼ cup pineapple juice
- 2 cloves garlic, minced
- 1 cup all-purpose flour
- 2 eggs, beaten
- Oil for frying
- 2 tablespoons oil, if needed
- Salt and pepper to taste

Directions:

1. Add the flour, salt, and pepper to a shallow dish and mix well. Dip the chicken pieces in the beaten egg followed by a dip in the flour to coat. Set aside.
2. Heat oil in a large skillet over medium-high heat. When hot, add the chicken pieces and cook until golden brown on all sides, about 6 minutes. You may have to work in batches, as you don't want the pieces to touch while cooking.
3. When done, remove the chicken from the skillet and place on a paper-towel-lined plate to drain excess oil.
4. If needed, add the rest of the oil to the skillet and heat over medium-high heat. When hot, add the onions, garlic, and peppers and cook until the onions and peppers start to soften.

5. When soft, return the chicken to the skillet along with the chili sauce, pineapple, and pineapple juice and allow to cook for about 7 minutes, stirring occasionally. Serve with a side of rice.

Nutrition:
624 Calories, 11g Fats, 31g Protein

My notes:

Boston Market's Meatloaf

Preparation Time: 10 minutes

Cooking Time: 1 hour 25 minutes

Servings: 8

Ingredients:

Sauce:

- 1 cup tomato sauce
- 1½ tablespoons barbecue sauce
- 1 tablespoon sugar

Meatloaf:

- 1½ pounds lean ground sirloin
- 6 tablespoons all-purpose flour
- ¾ teaspoon salt
- ½ teaspoon onion powder
- ¼ teaspoon ground black pepper
- 1 dash garlic powder

Directions:

1. Preheat the oven to 400F, and place the ground sirloin into a bowl.
2. Mix the sauce ingredients together and bring to a simmer over medium heat. When the sauce is simmering, remove it from heat. Set aside 2 tablespoons of the sauce and pour the rest over the meat. Massage the sauce into the meat, marinating it well.
3. Add the rest of the meatloaf ingredients into the meat mixture and continue mixing and kneading until the spices are fully incorporated into the meat. Place the meat into your loaf pan and cover with foil. Bake the meat mixture for 30 minutes.
4. Remove the pan from the oven and drain the fat before cutting the meatloaf into 8 equal portions.

5. Pour the set-aside sauce over the top of the meatloaf and return it to the oven for another 25 to 30 minutes. Transfer the meatloaf to a plate and let cool before serving.

Nutrition:

210.1 Calories, 10.9g Fats, 8.8g Carbs, 18.3g Protein

My notes:

Marinated Tuna Steak

Preparation Time: 10 minutes

Cooking Time: 15-20 minutes

Servings: 4

Ingredients:

- 2 tablespoons Olive oil
- ¼ cup Orange juice
- ¼ cup Soy sauce
- 1 tablespoon Lemon juice
- 2 tablespoons fresh parsley
- 1 Garlic clove
- 5 tablespoons ground black pepper
- 2 tablespoons fresh oregano
- 4 Oz. Tuna steaks

Directions:

1. Mince the garlic and chop the oregano and parsley.
2. In a glass container, mix the pepper, oregano, garlic, parsley, lemon juice, soy sauce, olive oil, and orange juice.
3. Warm the grill using the high heat setting. Grease the grate with oil. Add to tuna steaks and cook for five to six minutes. Turn and baste with the marinated sauce.
4. Cook another five minutes or until it's the way you like it. Discard the remaining marinade.

Nutrition:

200g. Calories, 27.4g. Protein, 79g. Fats

My notes:

Garlic and Shrimp Pasta

Preparation Time: 5 minutes

Cooking Time: 15 minutes

Servings: 4

Ingredients:

- 6 Oz. whole-wheat spaghetti
- 12 Oz. raw shrimp, peeled and deveined, cut into 1-inch pieces
- 1 bunch asparagus, trimmed
- 1 large bell pepper, thinly sliced
- 1 cup fresh peas
- 3 garlic cloves, chopped
- 1 and ¼ teaspoons kosher salt
- ½ and ½ cups non-fat plain yogurt
- 3 tablespoon lemon juice
- 1 tablespoon extra-virgin olive oil
- ½ teaspoon fresh ground black pepper
- ¼ cup pine nuts, toasted

Directions:

1. Take a large-sized pot and bring water to a boil. Add your spaghetti and cook them for about minutes less than the directed package instruction.
2. Add shrimp, bell pepper, asparagus and cook for about 2- 4 minutes until the shrimp are tender. Drain the pasta and the contents well

3. Take a large bowl and mash garlic until a paste form Whisk in yogurt, parsley, oil, pepper, and lemon juice into the garlic paste. Add pasta mixture and toss well.
4. Serve by sprinkling some pine nuts!

Nutrition:

406 Calories, 22 g Fats, 28g. Carbohydrates, 26g Protein

My notes:

PF Chang's Orange Peel Chicken

Preparation Time: 10 minutes

Cooking Time: 30 minutes

Servings: 4

Ingredients:

- 4 boneless, skinless chicken breasts
- ¾ cup flour
- ¼ cup orange peel from 1 orange
- 2 tablespoons cornstarch
- 2 tablespoons garlic, minced
- 2 teaspoons black pepper
- 2 teaspoons Creole seasoning
- 2 teaspoons garlic powder
- 2 teaspoons onion powder
- 1 teaspoon chili powder
- Extra-virgin olive oil
- Orange peel sauce
- 1 cup tomato sauce
- 6 tablespoons orange juice
- 6 tablespoons chicken broth
- ¼ cup brown sugar
- 2 tablespoons sriracha
- 1 tablespoon soy sauce
- 1 teaspoon chili paste
- ¼ teaspoon black pepper

Directions:

1. Peel and clean an orange, removing the white pulpy part and cutting out the segments which will be used for garnish. Julienne the peel and set aside with the segments. Stir together all the sauce ingredients in a mixing bowl. Set aside.
2. Cut the chicken into bite-sized cubes. In another bowl, mix together all the spices. Toss over the chicken pieces. Stir to make sure the chicken is properly covered.
3. In a small dish, stir together the flour and cornstarch. Pour over the seasoned chicken and stir again to make sure the chicken is coated.
4. Heat the olive oil in a large skillet over medium-high heat. When hot, stir in the chicken and cook until browned on all sides. You may have to work in batches to cook the chicken faster and more evenly. When all the chicken has been cooked, remove it from the skillet.
5. Add a bit more olive oil to the pan, then toss in the orange peel slices and the garlic and cook just until garlic is fragrant. Add the sauce to the skillet and bring to a boil, then reduce heat and cook for 5 minutes or until the sauce begins to thicken. Return the chicken to the skillet and cook for 5 more minutes. Garnish with orange segments and serve with rice.

Nutrition:

691 Calories, 10g Fats, 31g Protein

My notes:

PF Chang's Crispy Honey Chicken

Preparation Time; 20 minutes

Cooking Time: 2 hours

Servings: 4

Ingredients:

Chicken:

- 1-pound chicken breast, boneless, skinless, cut into medium-sized chunks
- Vegetable oil, for frying and deep-frying

Batter:

- 4 ounces all-purpose flour
- 2½ ounces cornstarch
- 1 egg
- 6 ounces water
- ⅛ teaspoon baking powder
- ⅛ teaspoon baking soda

Chicken seasoning:

- 1 tablespoon light soy sauce
- ⅛ teaspoon white pepper
- ¼ teaspoon kosher salt
- 1 tablespoon cornstarch

Sauce

- ½ cup sake or rice wine
- ½ cup honey
- 3 ounces rice vinegar
- 3 tablespoons light soy sauce
- 6 tablespoons sugar
- ¼ cup cornstarch
- ¼ cup water

Directions:

1. Make the batter at least 2 hours in advance. Mix all the batter ingredients together and refrigerate. After an hour and 40 minutes,

mix all the seasoning ingredients together and mix in the chicken. Make sure that the chicken is covered entirely.

2. Place the chicken in the refrigerator to marinate for at least 20 minutes. Mix all the sauce ingredients together - except the cornstarch and water - and set aside.
3. Before you begin frying your chicken:
4. Place a paper towel on a plate in preparation for draining the oil, and Heat your oil to 350F.
5. When your oil is heated, remove the chicken from the refrigerator and pour the batter all over it.
6. One by one, lower the coated chicken pieces into the heated oil. Keep them suspended until the batter is cooked, about 20 to 30 seconds.
7. When all the chicken is cooked, place it on the plate covered with the paper towel to cool and drain. Bring the sauce mixture to a boil. While waiting for it to boil, mix the cornstarch and water in a separate bowl.
8. Slowly pour the cornstarch mixture into the sauce and continue cooking for 2 minutes until the sauce thickens. When the sauce thickens, remove it from heat.
9. When the chicken is cooked, pour some sauce over the entire mixture, just enough to cover the chicken. Transfer everything to a plate with rice or Chinese noodles and serve.

Nutrition:

679 Calories, 12g Fats, 32g Protein

My notes:

PF Chang's Chicken Fried Rice

My notes:

Preparation Time: 10 minutes

Cooking Time: 10 minutes

Servings: 4

Ingredients:

- 2 cups prepared rice
- 1 chicken breast, cut into bite-sized Pieces and seasoned with salt & pepper
- ½ cup frozen mixed vegetables
- 2 green onions, chopped
- 1 clove garlic, minced
- 1 egg
- 3 teaspoons sesame or wok oil, divided
- 2 tablespoons soy sauce

Directions:

1. In a small dish, beat together the egg and 1 teaspoon of oil. In a large skillet or wok, heat another teaspoon of the oil and cook the chicken until done. Remove from skillet and set aside.
2. Add the last teaspoon of oil to the skillet and stir in the mixed vegetables and green onions. Cook and stir until hot and tender. Then add the garlic and cook until fragrant. Using a spatula or spoon, move the vegetables to one side. Add the egg mixture and scramble until cooked, then add the chicken and stir until it is all combined.

Nutrition:

641 Calories, 9g Fats, 34g Protein

Pei Wei's Spicy Chicken

Preparation Time: 10 minutes

Cooking Time: 15 minutes

Servings: 4

Ingredients:

- 2 boneless skinless chicken breasts, cut into 1-inch pieces
- 1½ cups sliced carrots
- 1½ cups sugar snap peas
- 3 cups vegetable oil for frying

Batter:

- 1½ cups flour
- 1½ teaspoons salt
- 1½ teaspoons baking soda
- 2 eggs
- ⅔ cup milk
- ⅔ cup water

Sauce:

- 3 teaspoons vegetable oil
- 3 tablespoons minced garlic
- ¼ cup green onion, chopped, white parts only
- 1½ cups pineapple juice
- 3 teaspoons chili garlic paste, more if you want it spicier
- 3 tablespoons white wine vinegar
- 2 tablespoons sugar
- 2 teaspoons soy sauce
- 1 teaspoon salt
- 4 teaspoons cornstarch
- 3 tablespoons water

Directions:

1. In a mixing bowl, stir together all the ingredients for the batter. It should be smooth and without lumps. It will be thinnish. In a saucepan, bring 3 cups of water to a boil, then add the carrots and

peas and cook just until tender. You want them to be a bit crispy. Drain and set aside.

2. In a deep pot or deep fryer, heat the 3 cups of oil to 375°F. Add the chicken to the hot oil a few pieces at a time. Leave it there until cooked through and golden brown, then transfer to a paper-towel-lined plate to drain.
3. In a large skillet or wok, heat 2 teaspoons of oil over medium-high heat. Add the garlic and green onion and cook for about 1 minute. In a bowl, stir together all the sauce ingredients except for the cornstarch and water.
4. Add the sauce mixture to the hot skillet and cook until it starts to bubble. Make a slurry of the cornstarch and water and add it to the bubbling sauce, and cook until the sauce starts to thicken. Add the chicken, peas, and carrots and cook until hot. Serve with rice.

Nutrition:
684 Calories, 9g Fats, 31g Protein

My notes:

Pei Wei's Chicken Pad Thai

Preparation Time: 15 minutes

Cooking Time: 15 minutes

Servings: 4 - 6

Ingredients:

- ½ cup low-fat coconut milk
- 6 tablespoons creamy peanut butter
- ¼ cup light soy sauce
- ¼ cup lime juice
- ½ tablespoon rice wine vinegar
- 2 tablespoons brown sugar
- 2 teaspoons grated ginger
- ½ teaspoon red pepper flakes
- Chicken stir-fry
- ½ tablespoon canola oil
- ½ tablespoon dark sesame oil
- 1–2 teaspoons curry powder (optional)
- 1-pound chicken breast, cut into bite-sized pieces
- 6–8 ounces frozen sugar snap peas
- 1 medium onion, chopped
- 2 cloves garlic, minced
- ½ pound cooked rice noodles or long thin pasta

Garnish:

- ¼ cup lightly salted dry roasted peanuts, chopped
- Cilantro

Directions:

1. Stir together all the sauce ingredients in a mixing bowl. Combine well, then set aside. Cook the noodles or pasta according to the package **Directions**. Set aside. Heat the canola oil and sesame oil in a large skillet over medium-high heat. When hot, add the chicken and stir. Allow to cook for about 5 minutes, then stir in the garlic.

2. When the chicken is completely cooked through, add the peas and cook a bit longer to heat the peas through. Stir in the sauce and make sure the chicken is evenly coated. Add the cooked noodles and stir to make sure everything is covered in the sauce. Serve with cilantro and top with chopped peanuts.

Nutrition:

612 Calories, 10g Fats, 33g Protein

My notes:

Stuffed Chicken Marsala

Preparation Time: 25 minutes

Cooking Time: 45 minutes

Servings: 4

Ingredients:

Chicken:

- 4 boneless skinless chicken breasts
- ¾ cup all-purpose flour
- Salt and pepper to taste
- ½ cup olive oil
- Parsley, chopped, for garnish

Stuffing:

- ½ cup smoked provolone or gouda cheese, shredded
- ½ pound mozzarella cheese, shredded
- ¼ cup parmesan cheese, grated
- ½ cup breadcrumbs
- 1 teaspoon fresh garlic, minced
- 1 teaspoon red pepper flakes
- 2 tablespoons sun-dried tomatoes, patted dry and roughly chopped
- 3 green onions, thinly sliced
- ¾ cup sour cream

Sauce:

- 1 yellow onion, sliced into strings
- 1-quart dry marsala wine
- 1 cup heavy cream
- ¾ pound button mushrooms, thinly sliced

Directions:

1. Combine all stuffing ingredients in a bowl. Set aside and preheat oven to 350°F. Make two slices at the thickest part of each chicken breast in order to butterfly it. Turn the chicken over and lay it flat. Cover with wax paper and pound to about ¼–½ inches in thickness.

2. Stuff each chicken breast, but do not overfill. Coat the chicken in salt, pepper, and flour. Cook the chicken in olive oil in a large skillet over medium-high heat. Once cooked, transfer to a baking dish and bake for 15–20 minutes or until the inside is cooked through.
3. Using the same large skillet, cook the onions in the chicken drippings for about 2 minutes. Add the mushrooms and continue to sauté for about 5 more minutes. Deglaze by adding wine to the skillet. Heat the wine until lightly bubbling to reduce it. Continue to cook until the sauce turns brown.
4. Heat the heavy cream in the microwave for 20 seconds. Pour it into the pan and heat until it bubbles slightly. Reduce heat to low and simmer for 5 minutes. Remove from heat when the sauce is a rich brown color.
5. Serve the sauce over the stuffed chicken and complement the meal with mashed potatoes, if desired. Sprinkle with chopped parsley.

Nutrition:

491 Calories, 4.6g Carbs, 31g Protein

My notes:

Chicken Margherita

Preparation Time: 35 minutes

Cooking Time: 25 minutes

Servings: 6

Ingredients:

Chicken:

- 6 (4-ounce) boneless chicken breasts
- 2 cups water
- ¼ cup salt
- ¼ cup sugar

Pesto:

- 2 cups fresh basil
- 1 clove garlic
- 2 tablespoons pecorino romano cheese, grated
- 3–4 tablespoons extra-virgin olive oil
- 1 tablespoon pine nuts (optional)
- Lemon garlic sauce
- 2 tablespoons butter
- 2 cloves garlic, minced
- 1 tablespoon all-purpose flour
- 1 tablespoon lemon juice
- ½ cup low-sodium chicken broth
- Chicken Margherita assembly
- 6 (4-ounce) grilled boneless chicken breasts
- ½ cup prepared pesto
- 1 cup grape tomatoes, halved
- 6 ounces fresh mozzarella, sliced
- ½ cup prepared lemon garlic sauce
- Freshly shredded parmesan cheese, for garnish

Directions:

1. In a Ziploc bag, combine the water, salt, and sugar. Mix well. Add the chicken and refrigerate for at least 2 hours.

2. Grill chicken until cooked thoroughly. Set aside. Blend all pesto ingredients in a food processor to achieve a smooth consistency. Add 1 tablespoon of oil, if needed. Refrigerate in a sealed container until ready to use.
3. To make the lemon garlic sauce, melt the butter in a small saucepan. Add garlic and sauté for 1 minute. Slowly add some flour and stir well. Add fresh lemon juice and chicken broth. Stir for about 3–5 minutes until the sauce begins to thicken. Keep refrigerated.
4. To assemble the Chicken Margherita, preheat oven to 425°F. Move the grilled chicken to a baking dish and top with mozzarella cheese, pesto, and halved grape tomatoes.
5. Pour the lemon garlic sauce on top. Bake until cheese melts, about 10–15 minutes. To serve, sprinkle with freshly grated parmesan cheese, if desired.

Nutrition:

469 Calories, 6.3g Carbs, 31g Protein

My notes:

Tuscan Garlic Chicken

Preparation Time: 15 minutes

Cooking Time: 30 minutes

Servings: 6

Ingredients:

Chicken:

- 1 cup all-purpose flour
- ½ cup panko bread crumbs
- 1 tablespoon garlic powder
- 2 teaspoons Italian seasoning
- 1 teaspoon sea salt
- ½ teaspoon ground black pepper
- ½ teaspoon dried basil
- ½ teaspoon dried oregano
- 3 boneless skinless chicken breasts (or 6 cutlets)
- 2 tablespoons olive oil

Pasta:

- 1-pound fettuccine

Sauce:

- 2 tablespoons unsalted butter
- 4 cloves garlic, minced
- 1 red bell pepper, cut into 2-inch-long thin strips
- ½ teaspoon sea salt
- ¼ teaspoon paprika
- ⅛ teaspoon ground black pepper
- 2 tablespoons all-purpose flour
- 1 cup low-sodium chicken broth
- 1 cup milk
- ½ cup half and half
- 2 cups fresh spinach, roughly chopped
- 1 cup freshly grated parmesan cheese

Directions:

1. Preheat oven to 400°F. Line a baking sheet with parchment paper. In a bowl, mix together flour, breadcrumbs, garlic powder, Italian seasoning, salt, pepper, basil, and oregano. Coat the chicken by tossing it in the mixture.
2. Heat the olive oil in a large skillet over medium heat. Carefully place the chicken in the oil. Sear for 2–3 minutes or until golden brown, making sure not to lose any of the coating. Place chicken onto a baking sheet and then into the oven for 15–20 minutes. While the chicken is baking, cook the fettuccine according to package instructions.
3. To make the sauce, melt the butter in a large skillet over medium-low heat. Add the bell pepper and cook for 3–4 minutes. Season with salt, pepper, and paprika, then add the garlic and sauté for about 1 minute.
4. Whisk in the flour, then slowly add the chicken broth, milk, and half and half. Bring the heat to medium and simmer. Add the spinach and cook until wilted. Let the sauce thicken and then mix in the parmesan cheese.
5. Remove from heat and stir until smooth. Place it in the fettuccine and toss together. Slice the chicken and place it in the fettuccine. Serve with extra parmesan cheese if desired.

Nutrition:

487 Calories, 34g Protein, 7.3g Carbs

My notes:

Pei Wei's Asian Diner Caramel Chicken

Preparation Time: 20 minutes

Cooking Time: 55 minutes

Servings: 6

Ingredients:

- 1 cup sugar
- ¼ cup water
- ¾ cup reduced-sodium chicken broth
- 3 tablespoons fish sauce
- 2 tablespoons soy sauce
- 1 whole chicken, cut into 10 pieces
- 1 teaspoon salt
- 2 tablespoons vegetable oil and more, if needed
- ¼ cup fresh ginger, chopped
- 2 tablespoons fresh garlic, chopped
- ½ large red onion, chopped
- 2 tablespoons jalapenos, chopped
- 1 English cucumber, sliced then julienned
- ½ red bell pepper, julienned lengthwise
- 1 carrot, cut diagonally
- 2 green onions, chopped
- ½ cup pineapple chunks
- ¼ cup fresh mint, chopped
- ¼ cup fresh cilantro, chopped

- ¼ cup fresh basil, chopped
- Cooked rice or rice vermicelli for serving
- Vietnamese vinaigrette
- ½ cup lime juice, plus wedges for serving
- ¼ cup light brown sugar
- 2 tablespoons Vietnamese fish sauce
- ½ teaspoon toasted sesame oil
- 4 teaspoons vegetable oil

Directions:

1. Preheat oven to 325°F. Combine sugar and water in a deep sauce pot. Bring to a boil and simmer until the sugar turns a dark caramel color. Do not let it burn, and do not stir the sugar while cooking, or it may crystallize.
2. Add the chicken broth. The broth will boil quickly and spatter because of the hot sugar, so be careful! This is the reason for the deep pot. Stir in the broth and continue stirring over low heat until the sugar dissolves. Add the fish sauce and soy sauce. Set aside.
3. Combine the Vietnamese vinaigrette ingredients in a medium bowl and add cucumbers, red bell peppers, and carrots. Marinate until ready to use. Season the chicken pieces with the salt.
4. Heat the vegetable oil in a large Dutch oven and brown the chicken pieces on all sides. Set aside. In the same pan, using the extra vegetable oil if needed, sauté the ginger, garlic, red onion, and jalapeno over medium heat for 4–5 minutes until soft and fragrant.
5. Add the browned chicken pieces and the caramel sauce to the Dutch oven, turning the chicken in the caramel broth to coat all sides. Arrange the chicken, so it is all submerged in the sauce as much as possible and bring to a boil.
6. Cover the pot, put in the oven, and braise until done, about 35–45 minutes. While the chicken is cooking, assemble the green onion, pineapple chunks, and the other herbs and set aside.

7. Just before serving, add the green onions and pineapple chunks and stir well. Serve the chicken over rice or rice vermicelli. Top with a portion of Vietnamese vinaigrette slaw.

Nutrition:

697 Calories, 12g Fats, 32g Protein

My notes:

Side Salad Recipes

House Salad and Dressing

Preparation Time: 10 minutes

Cooking Time: 0 minutes

Servings: 12

Ingredients:

Salad:

- 1 head iceberg lettuce
- ¼ small red onion, sliced thin
- 6–12 black olives, pitted
- 6 pepperoncini
- 2 small Roma tomatoes, sliced

Croutons:

- ¼ cup shredded or grated Romano or parmesan cheese Dressing
- 1 packet Italian dressing mix
- ¾ cup vegetable/canola oil
- ¼ cup olive oil
- 1 tablespoon mayonnaise
- ⅓ cup white vinegar
- ¼ cup water
- ½ teaspoon sugar
- ½ teaspoon dried Italian seasoning
- ½ teaspoon salt
- ¼ teaspoon pepper
- ¼ teaspoon garlic powder

Directions:

1. To make the dressing, combine all ingredients in a small bowl. Thoroughly whisk together. Refrigerate for 1 hour to marinate. Add the salad ingredient to a salad bowl. When ready to serve, add some of the dressing to the salad and toss to coat. Add grated cheese as a garnish as desired. Store remaining dressing in an airtight container. Keep refrigerated, and it can be stored for up to 3 weeks.

Nutrition:

435 Calories, 54.8g Fats, 46.4g Carbs, 13.9g Protein

My notes:

Santa Fe Crispers Salad

Preparation Time: 10 minutes

Cooking Time: 30 minutes

Servings: 4

Ingredients:

- ½ pounds boneless skinless chicken breasts
- 1 tablespoon fresh cilantro, chopped
- ¾ cup Lawry's Santa Fe Chili Marinated with Lime and Garlic, divided

  1 package (10 ounces) torn romaine lettuce, approximately 8 cups
- 2 tablespoons milk
- 1 cup black beans, drained and rinsed
- ½ cup sour cream
- 1 cup drained canned whole kernel corn
- ¼ cup red onion, chopped
- 1 medium avocado, cut into chunks
- ½ cup Monterey Jack, shredded
- 1 medium tomato, cut into chunks

Directions:

1. Place chicken in a large glass dish or re-sealable marinade plastic bag. Add approximately ½ cup of the Santa Fe marinade, turn several times until nicely coated
2. Refrigerate for 30 minutes or longer.
3. Removed the chicken from marinade; get rid of the leftover marinade. Grill the chicken until cooked through, for 6 to 7 minutes per side, over medium heat; brush with 2 tablespoons of the leftover marinade. Cut the chicken into thin slices.
4. Combine the sour cream together with milk, leftover marinade, and cilantro with wire whisk in a medium-sized bowl until smooth Arrange lettuce on large serving platter.

5. Top with the chicken, avocado, corn, beans, cheese, tomato, and onion.
6. Serve with tortilla chips and dressing. Enjoy.

Nutrition:

676 Calories, 86g Fats, 67g Carbs, 46g Protein

Quesadilla Explosion Salad

My notes:

Preparation Time: 20 minutes

Cooking Time: 20 minutes

Servings: 1

Ingredients:

- 1 vegetarian chicken patty
- 6 ounces bagged salad mix

For Chipotle Ranch Dressing:

- 1 cup 2% milk
- 1 packet ranch dressing mix
- 1 teaspoon chipotle peppers in adobo sauce
- 1 cup non-fat Greek yogurt

For Citrus Balsamic Vinaigrette

- 2 tablespoon balsamic vinegar
- ½ teaspoon orange zest
- 2 tablespoon Splenda
- ¼ cup orange juice
- A pinch of nutmeg

For Sweet Potato Strips:

- ¼ medium sweet potato, washed, thinly sliced & cut into strips nonstick cooking spray
- ¼ teaspoon salt

For Cheese Quesadilla:

- 1 mission carb balance whole wheat fajita sized tortilla 1 ounce reduced-fat Colby Jack cheese, shredded

For Roasted Corn and Black Bean Salsa:

- 1 cup black beans, rinsed
- 2 ears of corn, roasted, kernels removed from cob ½ cup fresh cilantro, chopped
- 1 tablespoon lime juice, freshly squeezed
- ¼ red onion, chopped
- 1 jalapeno pepper, roasted, peeled, seeded, de-veined & chopped Salt to taste

- 1 red bell pepper, medium, roasted, peeled, seeded & chopped

Directions:

For Sweet Potato Strips:

1. Preheat oven to 350 F. Lightly coat the strips with nonstick cooking spray and then dust them lightly with the salt. Place on a large-sized cookie sheet in a single layer & bake for 15 to 20 minutes. Don't forget to stir the strips & turn halfway during the baking process.
2. Set aside and let cool until ready to use.

For Roasted Corn Salsa:

3. Add corn together with peppers & black beans to a large bowl and then squeeze the lime juice on top; add salt to taste. Give the ingredients a good stir & add the fresh cilantro.

For Chipotle Ranch Dressing:

4. Add yogurt and milk to the ranch dressing mix. Stir in the chipotle & store in a refrigerator.

For Citrus Balsamic Vinaigrette:

5. Over low heat in a large saucepan; place the entire ingredients together & cook for a minute. Set aside and let cool, then refrigerate.

For Quesadilla:

6. Place the cheese on half of the tortilla & then fold over.
7. Lightly coat the tortilla with the nonstick cooking spray & then cook over medium-high heat in a large pan. Cook until the cheese is completely melted, for a minute per side. Cut into 4 wedges.
8. Prepare the veggie "chicken" patty as per the Directions mentioned on the package & then slice into thin strips.
9. Place approximately 6 ounces of the salad mix on the plate and then top with the "chicken" strips, black bean salsa, sweet potato strips & roasted corn.
10. Place the cut quesadilla around the edge of the plate and then drizzle the salad with the prepared dressings.

Nutrition:

245 Calories, 59.8g Fats, 67.3g Carbs, 12.8g Protein

Caribbean Shrimp Salad

Preparation Time: 20 minutes

Cooking Time: 55 minutes

Servings: 4

Ingredients:

- 8 cups baby spinach, fresh
- ¼ cup lime juice, freshly squeezed
- 2 tablespoons chili garlic sauce
- ½ teaspoon paprika
- 4 cups cooked shrimp
- 5 tablespoons seasoned rice vinegar, divided
- ½ teaspoon ground cumin
- 1 cup peeled mango, chopped
- ½ cup green onions, thinly sliced
- 2 garlic cloves, minced
- 1 cup radishes, julienne-cut
- ¼ cup peeled avocado, diced
- 2 tablespoons pumpkinseed kernels, unsalted 1 ½ tablespoons olive oil
- Dash of salt

Directions:

1. In a large bowl; combine the cooked shrimp together with chili garlic sauce & 2 tablespoons of vinegar; toss well.
2. Cover & let chill for an hour.
3. Now, in a small bowl, combine the leftover vinegar together with garlic cloves, oil, lime juice, lime rind, ground cumin, paprika & salt, stirring well with a whisk.

4. Place 2 cups of spinach on each of 4 plates; top each serving with a cup of the prepared shrimp mixture. Arrange ¼ cup radishes, ¼ cup mango & 1 tablespoon of the avocado around the shrimp on each plate.
   Top each serving with approximately 1 ½ teaspoons of pumpkinseed kernels & 2 tablespoons of green onions. Drizzle each salad with approximately 2 tablespoons of the vinaigrette. Serve and enjoy.

Nutrition:

124 Calories, 76.9g Fats, 67.9g Carbs, 45.8g Protein

My notes:

Southwest Caesar Salad

My notes:

Preparation Time: 10 minutes

Cooking Time: 20 minutes

Servings: 6

Ingredients:

- 2 tablespoons mayonnaise
- ¼ teaspoon cayenne or... ground red pepper
- 6 cups fresh romaine lettuce, washed
- ⅓ cup parmesan cheese, grated
- 1 cup croutons
- ½ of a red bell pepper, cut into thin strips
- 1 cup whole kernel corn, frozen & thawed
- ½ cup fresh cilantro, chopped
- 2 tablespoons green onion, chopped
- ¼ cup olive oil
- 2 tablespoon lime juice, freshly squeezed
- 1/8 teaspoon salt

Directions:

1. Place onions together with mayo, ground red pepper, lime juice, and salt in a blender or food processor; cover & process until blended well. Slowly add the oil at the top using the feed tube & continue to process after each addition until blended well.
2. Toss the lettuce with the corn, croutons, bell peppers, cheese, and cilantro in a large bowl.
3. Add the mayo mixture; evenly toss until nicely coated. Serve immediately & enjoy.

Nutrition:

265 Calories, 62g Fats, 98g Carbs, 47g Protein

Red Beans from Popeye's

Preparation Time: 20 minutes

Cooking Time: 40 minutes

Servings: 10

My notes:

Ingredients:

- 3 14-ounce cans red beans
- ¾ pounds smoked ham hock
- 1¼ cups water
- ½ teaspoon onion powder
- ½ teaspoon garlic salt
- ¼ teaspoon red pepper flakes
- ½ teaspoon salt
- 3 tablespoons lard
- Steamed long-grain rice

Directions:

1. Add 2 canned red beans, ham hock, and water to the pot. Cook on medium heat and let simmer for about 1 hour.
2. Remove from heat and wait until the meat is cool enough to handle. Then remove meat from the bone.
3. In a food processor, add meat, cooked red beans and water mixture, onion powder, garlic salt, red pepper, salt, and lard. Pulse for 4 seconds. You want the beans to be cut, and the liquid thickened. Drain the remaining 1 can red beans and add to the food processor. Pulse for only 1 or 2 seconds.
4. Remove ingredients from the food processor and transfer to the pot from earlier.
5. Cook on low heat, stirring frequently until mixture is heated through. Serve over steamed rice.

Nutrition:

445 Calories, 12g Fats, 67g Carbs, 9g Fibers

Café Rio's Sweet Pork Barbacoa Salad

Preparation Time: 10 minutes

Cooking Time: 8 minutes

Servings: 8

Ingredients:

- 3 pounds pork loin
- Garlic salt, to taste
- 1 can root beer
- ¼ cup water
- ¾ cup brown sugar
- 1 10-ounce can red enchilada sauce
- 1 4-ounce can green chilies
- ½ teaspoon chili powder
- 8 large burrito size tortillas
- 1½ serving Cilantro Lime Rice
- 1 can black beans, drained and heated
- 2 heads Romaine lettuce, shredded
- 1½ cups tortilla strips
- 1 cup Queso Fresco cheese
- 2 limes, cut in wedges
- ¼ cup cilantro

Dressing:

- ½ packet Hidden Valley Ranch Dressing Mix 1 cup mayonnaise
- ½ cup milk
- ½ cup cilantro leaves
- ¼ cup salsa Verde
- ½ jalapeno pepper, deseeded
- 1 plump clove garlic
- 2 tablespoons fresh lime juice

Directions:

1. Sprinkle garlic salt on pork. Put in the slow cooker with the flat side facing down.

2. Add ¼ cup root beer and water. Cover and cook on low setting for 6 hours.
3. To prepare sauce, add the rest of the root beer, brown sugar, enchilada sauce, green chilies, and chili powder in a blender. Blend until smooth.
4. Remove meat from slow cooker then transfer onto the cutting board. Shred, discarding juices and fat. Return shredded pork to slow cooker with the sauce.
5. Cook on low setting for another 2 hours.
6. When there is only about 15 to 20 minutes left to cook, remove the lid to thicken the sauce.
7. To prepare the dressing, mix all dressing ingredients in a blender. Puree until smooth. Then, transfer to the refrigerator and allow to chill for at least 1 hour.
8. To assemble the salad, layer tortilla, rice, beans, pork, lettuce, tortilla strips, cheese, and dressing in a bowl. Serve with a lime wedge and cilantro leaves.

Nutrition:

756 Calories, 28g Fats, 91g Carbs, 7g Fibers

My notes:

My notes:

Delicious ideas for kids

Have you ever had the experience that you cooked for a long time and then your child did not want to eat?
Even their big guests are happy about lovingly prepared dishes.

Here are some suggestions:

Practical Advice for Beginners to Canning and Preserving your favorite Foods

There are a few safety tips that you should follow when you start canning and preserving foods from home. Canning is a great way to store and preserve foods, but it can be risky if not done correctly. However, if you follow these tips, you will be able to can foods safely.

Choose the Right Canner

The first step to safe home canning is choosing the right canner. First off, know when to use a pressure canner or a water bath canner.
Use a pressure canner that is specifically designed for canning and preserving foods. There are several types of canner out there, and some are just for cooking food, not for preserving food and processing jars. Be sure that you have the right type of equipment.

Make sure your pressure canner is the right size. If your canner is too small, the jars may be undercooked. Always opt for a larger canner as the pressure on the bigger pots tends to be more accurate, and you will be able to take advantage of the larger size and can more foods at once!

Before you begin canning, check that your pressure canner is in good condition. If your canner has a rubber gasket, it should be flexible and soft. If the rubber is dry or cracked, it should be replaced before you start canning. Be sure your canner is clean, and the small vents in the lid are free of debris. Adjust your canner for high altitude processing if needed.

Once you are sure your canner is ready to go and meets all these guidelines, it is time to start canning!

Opt for a Screw Top Lid System

There are many kinds of canning jars that you can choose to purchase. However, the only type of jar approved by the USDA is a mason jar with a screw-top lid. These are designated "preserving jars" and are considered the safest and most effective option for home preserving uses.

Some jars are not thought to be safe for home preservation despite being marketed as canning jars. Bail Jars, for example, have a two-part wire clasp lid with a rubber ring in between the lid and jar. While these were popular in the past, it is now thought that the thick rubber and tightly closed lid does not provide a sufficient seal, leading to a higher potential for botulism. Lightening Jars should not be used for canning as they are simply glass jars with glass lids, with no rubber at all. That will not create a good seal!

Reusing jars from store-bought products is another poor idea. They may look like they're in good condition, but they are typically designed to be processed in a commercial facility. Most store-bought products do not have the two-part band and lid system, which is best for home canning. The rubber seal on a store-bought product is likely not reusable once you open the original jar. You can reuse store-bought jars at home for storage but not for canning and preserving.

Check Your Jars, Lids, and Bands

As you wash your jars with soapy water, check for any imperfections. Even new jars may have a small chip or crack and need to be discarded. You can reuse jars again and again as long as they are in good condition.
The metal jar rings are also reusable; however, you should only reuse them if they are rust free and undented. If your bands begin to show signs of wear, consider investing in some new ones.

Jar lids need to be new as the sealing compound on the lid can disintegrate over time. When you store your jars in damp places (like in a basement or canning cellar), the lids are even more likely to disintegrate. Always use new lids to ensure that your canning is successful.

Check for Recent Canning Updates

Canning equipment has changed over the years, becoming higher-tech and, therefore, more efficient at processing foods. In addition to the equipment becoming more advanced, there have also been many scientific improvements, making canning safer when the proper steps are taken. For example, many people used to sterilize their jars before pressure canning. While this is still okay to do, it is unnecessary as science has shown that any bacteria in the jars will die when heated to such a high temperature in a pressure canner. Sterilization is an extra step that you don't need!
Make sure that your food preservation information is all up to date and uses current canning guidelines. Avoid outdated cookbooks and reassess "trusted family methods" to make sure they fit into the most recent criteria for safe canning. When in doubt, check with the US Department of Agriculture's Complete Guide to Home Canning, which contains the most recent, up-to-date canning tips.

Pick the Best Ingredients

When choosing food to can, always get the best food possible. You want to use high quality, perfectly ripe produce for canning. You will never end up with a jar of food better than the product itself, so picking good ingredients is important to your final product's taste. Also, products that past their prime can affect the ability to handle it. If strawberries are overripe, your jam may come out too runny. If your tomatoes are past their prime, they may not have a high enough pH level to be processed in a water bath. Pick your ingredients well, and you will make successfully preserved foods.

Clean everything

While you may know that your jars and lids need to be washed and sanitized, don't forget about the rest of your tools. Cleaning out your canner before using it is essential, even if you put it away clean. Make sure to wipe your countertop well, making sure there are no crumbs or residue. Wash your produce with clean, cold water, and don't forget to wash your hands! The cleaner everything is, the less likely you are to spread bacteria onto your jarred foods.

Follow Your Recipe

Use recipes from trusted sources, and be sure to follow them to the letter. Changing the amount of one or two ingredients may alter the balance of acidity and result in unsafe canning (especially when using a water bath canner). Use the ingredients as directed and make very few changes—none if possible.

Adhere to the processing times specified by your recipe. Sometimes the times may seem a little long, but the long processing time makes these products safe to store on the shelf. The processing time is the correct amount of time needed to destroy spoilage organisms, mold spores, yeast, and pathogens in the jar. So, as you may have guessed, it is extremely important to use the times written in your recipe as a hard rule.

Cool the Jars

Be sure that you give your jars 12 hours to cool before testing the seal. If you test the seal too early, it may break as the jar is still warm, making it pliable. Be sure to cool the jars away from a window or fan as even a slight breeze may cause the hot jars to crack. Once cool, remove the metal band, clean it and save it for your next canning project.

Conclusion

Dear Reader,
We're on the last few pages of this book, and I'd like to ask you how much you enjoyed flipping through it.
Did you find any new recipes for your lunch and dinner?
Did you enjoy them on your own or with someone else?
And what did you think of the suggestions in the children's pages?

Maybe you've chosen from the index the recipes you've heard of before or those recipes that remind you of something you've already eaten with family and friends. Maybe you'll want to try all the recipes in this book.

... Take your time.

While you were reading, you probably also noticed how many and what dishes you can combine to surprise your guests, or maybe you found recipes that would taste better by changing a few ingredients and adding your personal touch.
Did you jot down your ideas in the notes section next to the recipes?
Have you noted in the tab below which page your favorite recipes are on?

Whether you're good in the kitchen or not, the recipes in this book are easy to prepare, don't require too many ingredients, and will allow you to recreate new masterworks every day that you, your family, and your guests will love.

A reason I sought out so-called "secret recipes" is the fact that once I found my favorite ones, I could enjoy them and combine them whenever I wanted to in the comfort of my own home.

Imagine being able to surprise your friends and family each time with the food they enjoyed the most at various restaurants.

Imagine how satisfying it would be to show them that you created those masterworks in the comfort of your kitchen with these copycat recipes!

If you're in the mood for more tasty, easy-to-prepare recipes, contact your local bookseller and don't miss our upcoming cookbooks.

Also, by Gordon Benedict Richman & Ernest D.W.:

Copycat Breakfast Cookbook for Beginners:
fifty easy and delicious morning meal recipes to recreate and enjoy with your family.

Copycat Lunch & Dinner Recipes for Beginners:
Improve your culinary skills with these tastiest dishes to combine or re-adapt to your taste.

Little Copycat Recipes Cookbook:
Recreate all these 50 dishes from the most popular restaurants, even if you are a beginner.

Copycat delicious meals Cookbook for beginners:
Prepare and choose from these 50 tasty dishes which one will be your Favorites.

Where are your sweetheart recipes?

Title **Page**

CPSIA information can be obtained
at www.ICGtesting.com
Printed in the USA
BVHW091042260521
608177BV00009B/886

9 781802 945201